THE COMPLETE
RUNNER'S

DAY-BY-DAY LOG
2009 CALENDAR

**Andrews McMeel
Publishing, LLC**

Kansas City

MARTY JEROME

2008

January
S	M	T	W	T	F	S
		1	2	3	4	5
6	7	8	9	10	11	12
13	14	15	16	17	18	19
20	21	22	23	24	25	26
27	28	29	30	31		

February
S	M	T	W	T	F	S
					1	2
3	4	5	6	7	8	9
10	11	12	13	14	15	16
17	18	19	20	21	22	23
24	25	26	27	28	29	

March
S	M	T	W	T	F	S
						1
2	3	4	5	6	7	8
9	10	11	12	13	14	15
16	17	18	19	20	21	22
23	24	25	26	27	28	29
30	31					

April
S	M	T	W	T	F	S
		1	2	3	4	5
6	7	8	9	10	11	12
13	14	15	16	17	18	19
20	21	22	23	24	25	26
27	28	29	30			

May
S	M	T	W	T	F	S
				1	2	3
4	5	6	7	8	9	10
11	12	13	14	15	16	17
18	19	20	21	22	23	24
25	26	27	28	29	30	31

June
S	M	T	W	T	F	S
1	2	3	4	5	6	7
8	9	10	11	12	13	14
15	16	17	18	19	20	21
22	23	24	25	26	27	28
29	30					

July
S	M	T	W	T	F	S
		1	2	3	4	5
6	7	8	9	10	11	12
13	14	15	16	17	18	19
20	21	22	23	24	25	26
27	28	29	30	31		

August
S	M	T	W	T	F	S
					1	2
3	4	5	6	7	8	9
10	11	12	13	14	15	16
17	18	19	20	21	22	23
24	25	26	27	28	29	30
31						

September
S	M	T	W	T	F	S
	1	2	3	4	5	6
7	8	9	10	11	12	13
14	15	16	17	18	19	20
21	22	23	24	25	26	27
28	29	30				

October
S	M	T	W	T	F	S
			1	2	3	4
5	6	7	8	9	10	11
12	13	14	15	16	17	18
19	20	21	22	23	24	25
26	27	28	29	30	31	

November
S	M	T	W	T	F	S
						1
2	3	4	5	6	7	8
9	10	11	12	13	14	15
16	17	18	19	20	21	22
23	24	25	26	27	28	29
30						

December
S	M	T	W	T	F	S
	1	2	3	4	5	6
7	8	9	10	11	12	13
14	15	16	17	18	19	20
21	22	23	24	25	26	27
28	29	30	31			

2010

January
S	M	T	W	T	F	S
					1	2
3	4	5	6	7	8	9
10	11	12	13	14	15	16
17	18	19	20	21	22	23
24	25	26	27	28	29	30
31						

February
S	M	T	W	T	F	S
	1	2	3	4	5	6
7	8	9	10	11	12	13
14	15	16	17	18	19	20
21	22	23	24	25	26	27
28						

March
S	M	T	W	T	F	S
	1	2	3	4	5	6
7	8	9	10	11	12	13
14	15	16	17	18	19	20
21	22	23	24	25	26	27
28	29	30	31			

April
S	M	T	W	T	F	S
				1	2	3
4	5	6	7	8	9	10
11	12	13	14	15	16	17
18	19	20	21	22	23	24
25	26	27	28	29	30	

May
S	M	T	W	T	F	S
						1
2	3	4	5	6	7	8
9	10	11	12	13	14	15
16	17	18	19	20	21	22
23	24	25	26	27	28	29
30	31					

June
S	M	T	W	T	F	S
		1	2	3	4	5
6	7	8	9	10	11	12
13	14	15	16	17	18	19
20	21	22	23	24	25	26
27	28	29	30			

July
S	M	T	W	T	F	S
				1	2	3
4	5	6	7	8	9	10
11	12	13	14	15	16	17
18	19	20	21	22	23	24
25	26	27	28	29	30	31

August
S	M	T	W	T	F	S
1	2	3	4	5	6	7
8	9	10	11	12	13	14
15	16	17	18	19	20	21
22	23	24	25	26	27	28
29	30	31				

September
S	M	T	W	T	F	S
			1	2	3	4
5	6	7	8	9	10	11
12	13	14	15	16	17	18
19	20	21	22	23	24	25
26	27	28	29	30		

October
S	M	T	W	T	F	S
					1	2
3	4	5	6	7	8	9
10	11	12	13	14	15	16
17	18	19	20	21	22	23
24	25	26	27	28	29	30
31						

November
S	M	T	W	T	F	S
	1	2	3	4	5	6
7	8	9	10	11	12	13
14	15	16	17	18	19	20
21	22	23	24	25	26	27
28	29	30				

December
S	M	T	W	T	F	S
			1	2	3	4
5	6	7	8	9	10	11
12	13	14	15	16	17	18
19	20	21	22	23	24	25
26	27	28	29	30	31	

2009

January

S	M	T	W	T	F	S
				1	2	3
4	5	6	7	8	9	10
11	12	13	14	15	16	17
18	19	20	21	22	23	24
25	26	27	28	29	30	31

February

S	M	T	W	T	F	S
1	2	3	4	5	6	7
8	9	10	11	12	13	14
15	16	17	18	19	20	21
22	23	24	25	26	27	28

March

S	M	T	W	T	F	S
1	2	3	4	5	6	7
8	9	10	11	12	13	14
15	16	17	18	19	20	21
22	23	24	25	26	27	28
29	30	31				

April

S	M	T	W	T	F	S
			1	2	3	4
5	6	7	8	9	10	11
12	13	14	15	16	17	18
19	20	21	22	23	24	25
26	27	28	29	30		

May

S	M	T	W	T	F	S
					1	2
3	4	5	6	7	8	9
10	11	12	13	14	15	16
17	18	19	20	21	22	23
24	25	26	27	28	29	30
31						

June

S	M	T	W	T	F	S
	1	2	3	4	5	6
7	8	9	10	11	12	13
14	15	16	17	18	19	20
21	22	23	24	25	26	27
28	29	30				

July

S	M	T	W	T	F	S
			1	2	3	4
5	6	7	8	9	10	11
12	13	14	15	16	17	18
19	20	21	22	23	24	25
26	27	28	29	30	31	

August

S	M	T	W	T	F	S
						1
2	3	4	5	6	7	8
9	10	11	12	13	14	15
16	17	18	19	20	21	22
23	24	25	26	27	28	29
30	31					

September

S	M	T	W	T	F	S
		1	2	3	4	5
6	7	8	9	10	11	12
13	14	15	16	17	18	19
20	21	22	23	24	25	26
27	28	29	30			

October

S	M	T	W	T	F	S
				1	2	3
4	5	6	7	8	9	10
11	12	13	14	15	16	17
18	19	20	21	22	23	24
25	26	27	28	29	30	31

November

S	M	T	W	T	F	S
1	2	3	4	5	6	7
8	9	10	11	12	13	14
15	16	17	18	19	20	21
22	23	24	25	26	27	28
29	30					

December

S	M	T	W	T	F	S
		1	2	3	4	5
6	7	8	9	10	11	12
13	14	15	16	17	18	19
20	21	22	23	24	25	26
27	28	29	30	31		

INTRODUCTION

Whether you acknowledge it or not, running tells a story about you. Invariably, it reveals depth of character, faith, grit, fear, and your various abilities to manage the unpredictable. With every workout, a little more of this tale is told. You can change some of the plot line through planned application or willful desire. Some of it unfolds against your best wishes, without any help or interference from you. Much of the story will always be a mystery. So it's not surprising that we should seek to find something of ourselves in the stories of other runners.

Captain David Rozelle has a story for you. A veteran of the war in Iraq, he lost his foot in a roadside bombing. Sixteen months later, he ran the New York City Marathon. Two marathons and ten triathlons after that, he signed up for a second tour of duty, becoming the first American soldier in history to return to battle in a war that claimed a limb. After dispensing with that small chore, he persuaded the army to grant him a highly unusual two-year post at Walter Reed Hospital as the senior administrative officer for amputee care. Rozelle wanted to create a radical rehab program that used competitive sports to return soldiers to normal life: running, surfing, rock climbing, bike racing, skiing, kayaking, and the like.

Advances in prosthesis have allowed amputees to set their sights much higher today than even 15 years ago. But the psychological barriers to recovery remain intransigent, often insurmountable. Rozelle believed that if you dangled a seemingly impossible goal in front of a determined athlete, psychological barriers would fall away. His hunch is reaping results. A small revolution is now underway in military hospitals for amputees: virtual-reality rooms to practice skiing and sailing, pools for kayaking, and 3-D gait labs that allow physicians to correct stride and customize prostheses. Many of these innovations were inspired by the results Rozelle got from injured athletes in his care. Today he regularly sponsors recovering soldiers in running events, bicycle races, and ski trips.

He's become something of a celebrity in and out of military circles: interviews on CNN; a movie deal for his memoir, *Back in Action*; offers to run for public office. But Rozelle shows less interest in celebrating his own heroics than in the men and women who share part of his story. Every year he takes a team of limb-loss patients from Walter Reed to the New York City Marathon. He has knocked more than two hours off his first finish time with a prosthetic foot. All runners believe that there are parts of us that are indomitable. David Rozelle demonstrates that the hardest obstacles we face are sometimes simply the diminished expectations of others.

External challenges such as physical disability can be taken to task with methodical determination. Internal challenges, on the other hand, can defeat not only a runner, but a life. This is especially true with clinical depression. It's hard for most runners to understand Lisa Smith-Batchen's inner struggles. After all, the distance champion ran four 100-mile races *and* the 135-mile Badwater Ultramarathon, which stretches across Death Valley in blistering summer heat—all in just 10 weeks. She was already a two-time champion of Badwater and the only woman to win the Marathon des Sables, a brutal six-day race across the Sahara.

The fierce dedication these types of events require in training alone runs counter to the listless psychological abyss we associate with depression. In fact, growing evidence shows that running isn't just good therapy for fighting depression; it might be the best. Clinical evidence has been pouring in for years, first from psycho-therapy, and now from medical schools, which are beginning to unravel the chemical changes in the brain that bring on depression. Duke University Medical School produced a study in 1999 that showed that running therapy was as effective as drugs for fighting depression in the short term. And it's *more* effective than drugs in the long term.

Yet here's the paradox: when clinical depression strikes, you lose all motivation to run. Smith-Batchen often found that she couldn't even get out of bed for days at a time. Her thoughts turned suicidal. But she found that coaching other runners inspired her. Brisk walks in the woods turned to short runs, which turned into harder training. Little by little, the light returned. Running isn't a perfect solution to depression: It treats the symptoms, but you must take care that you're not simply running away from the causes, as more than one therapist

has explained it. And even after you've returned to normal living, depression can strike again at any time, often without warning. As Lisa Smith-Batchen discovered, however, there's hope for those who can find their way back to a training program.

There's an entirely different kind of hope for aging runners (which, alas, includes you). Nearly 43 percent of marathoners this year will be 40 or older. This statistic would have been unimaginable in, say, 1970. Certainly, our population is aging and we're leading healthier lives. We also know a lot more about training smart. But our abilities as athletes, as human beings, continue to vault ahead of the cautious optimism of science. Consider that Dimitrion Yordandis (98 years old) and Jenny Wood Allen (91 years old) recently became the oldest man and the oldest woman to complete a marathon.

Even more impressive is Terry Stanley, a 53-year-old elementary school principal, who not only finishes marathons—but wins them. He has won the Presque Isle event in Erie, Pennsylvania, twice. What's unique is that those victories were 28 years apart. To be sure, he's slowed a little in the past quarter century. His time in 1977 (when he was 25) was 2:23:13. His time in 2005 was 2:46:38. What is his secret? Training—consistent, realistic, and patient. His first workout of the day begins before dawn, just as it did when he was in his twen-ties. His second workout comes after work. The results speak for themselves. And as a runner, so does his story.—Marty Jerome ■

January

SUNDAY	MONDAY	TUESDAY	WEDNESDAY	THURSDAY	FRIDAY	SATURDAY
				1 New Year's Day Kwanzaa ends (USA)	2 Bank Holiday (Scotland)	3
4	5	6	7	8	9	10
11	12	13	14	15	16	17
18	19 Martin Luther King Jr.'s Birthday (observed) (USA)	20	21	22	23	24
25	26 Australia Day	27	28	29	30	31

"Growth demands a temporary surrender of security."

—Gail Sheehy

EDUCATION

If it's true that we learn more from failure than from success, I am a scholar at running. My boo-boos would be fewer if I could learn the secret to setting good goals. I set bad ones. As you contemplate where you want your training program to take you in the coming year, perhaps my blunders can help educate your ambitions.

The most common mistake all athletes make is in letting last year's goals dictate this year's. The paradox of training is that the fitter you get, the less room you have to improve. Sooner or later you'll hit the limits of your abilities or of age. If last year brought great leaps in improvement for speed, distance, weight loss, or any other yardstick for running, you'll want to refine or change your sights this year.

This brings up a second common mistake: the failure to bring your goals up for periodic review. Ultimately, training is about change, not only in your performance, but in your physical being, your desires, and your essential abilities. You will be a different person in July than you are in January. Your goals should accommodate this new you in all of its nuances. Any competitive event makes a good time to reassess. If you don't compete, plan to revisit your goals at least twice a year. Thrice-annual reviews are even better.

While you're at it, don't confuse dreams with goals. Running the Maui Marathon, dropping 20 pounds, achieving a new personal best time in your charity's 10K event are dreams. The workouts that will make these dreams happen should be your goals. They're the progressive reality you'll confront every time you put on your running shoes. Over the weeks and months they'll show you little by little whether or not your dreams are within reach. Goals are specific: times, distances, sets, workouts in a week. They can be measured and counted.

But don't let them become a tyranny. Even Olympic runners have plateaus and lingering dips in performance that arrive and leave with mysterious caprice. There will always be unforeseen demands on your time. The flu doesn't care about a nearing marathon date. Your job will invariably grow more demanding at a terrible time. Setbacks are inevitable and the discipline and focus that good goals require also need a little humanity. Otherwise, your training plans are likely to go up in smoke.

Meanwhile, it helps to hedge your bets. Diversifying your goals—changing speed to distance goals, for example, or developing your skills as a trail runner while also training for a street race—may sound like you're planning for failure. Quite the opposite: variable challenges keep enthusiasm alive. They also help reveal your true talents as a runner.

Finally, be willing to seek help if you're struggling. Help comes in many forms: coaches, the support of a running club, the companionship of a running partner (including the kind that run on four feet), even Internet chat rooms. A few words from kindred runners can keep you right on track. ∎

Distance carried forward: _____

29 Monday

_____
_____

Where & When: _____ **Distance:** _____
Comments: _____
_____

30 Tuesday

_____
_____

Where & When: _____ **Distance:** _____
Comments: _____
_____

31 Wednesday

_____
_____

Where & When: _____ **Distance:** _____
Comments: _____
_____

1 Thursday   1

_____
_____

Where & When: _____ **Distance:** _____
Comments: _____
_____

2 Friday   2

_____
_____

Where & When: _____ **Distance:** _____
Comments: _____
_____

Dec 2008/Jan

3   Saturday **3**

Where & When: **Distance:**

Comments:

4   Sunday **4**

Where & When: **Distance:**

Comments:

© Anthony West/CORBIS

tip: To raise your mileage, run longer distances in your regular workouts. Don't add more workouts to your week.

Distance this week: **Weight:**

5 Monday 5

Where & When: Distance:

Comments:

6 Tuesday 6

Where & When: Distance:

Comments:

7 Wednesday 7

Where & When: Distance:

Comments:

8 Thursday 8

Where & When: Distance:

Comments:

9 Friday 9

Where & When: Distance:

Comments:

January

Saturday **10**

Where & When: Distance:

Comments:

Sunday **11**

Where & When: Distance:

Comments:

© Ted Levine/zefa/CORBIS

tip: Don't lean too far forward when running up a hill. It reduces breathing capacity and restricts your natural leg motion.

Distance this week: **Weight:**

Distance carried forward: _____

12 Monday 12
_____

Where & When: _____ **Distance:** _____
Comments: _____
_____

13 Tuesday 13
_____

Where & When: _____ **Distance:** _____
Comments: _____
_____

14 Wednesday 14
_____

Where & When: _____ **Distance:** _____
Comments: _____
_____

15 Thursday 15
_____

Where & When: _____ **Distance:** _____
Comments: _____
_____

16 Friday 16
_____

Where & When: _____ **Distance:** _____
Comments: _____
_____

January

17

Where & When: Distance:

Comments:

18

Where & When: Distance:

Comments:

© Mika/zefa/CORBIS

tip: Schedule your runs in writing. Putting "Run" into a specific time slot on your calendar empowers the moment. You're more likely to follow through.

Distance this week: **Weight:**

Distance carried forward:

19 Monday   19

Where & When: **Distance:**

Comments:

---

20 Tuesday   20

Where & When: **Distance:**

Comments:

---

21 Wednesday   21

Where & When: **Distance:**

Comments:

---

22 Thursday   22

Where & When: **Distance:**

Comments:

---

23 Friday   23

Where & When: **Distance:**

Comments:

January

Saturday 24

Where & When: Distance:

Comments:

Sunday 25

Where & When: Distance:

Comments:

© Michael DeYoung/CORBIS

tip: When running in freezing weather, multiple thin layers work best. And if you tend to overdress because you don't like feeling cold in the early going, throw your clothes in the dryer for a few minutes before leaving the house.

Distance this week: Weight:

Distance carried forward:

26 Monday

Where & When: **Distance:**

Comments:

27 Tuesday

Where & When: **Distance:**

Comments:

28 Wednesday

Where & When: **Distance:**

Comments:

29 Thursday

Where & When: **Distance:**

Comments:

30 Friday

Where & When: **Distance:**

Comments:

Jan/Feb

31   **Saturday 31**

Where & When: **Distance:**

Comments:

32   **Sunday 1**

Where & When: **Distance:**

Comments:

tip:

Goals are specific. You can measure them, and they have a concrete time frame. Everything else is just a prayer of good intention.

tip: When starting over, give yourself 8 to 12 weeks to build an aerobic base before you add speed work to your routine.

tip: If you run on a track, train on the outside lanes. Wider turns are easier on ankles and feet.

Notes:

Distance this week: **Weight:**

February

SUNDAY	MONDAY	TUESDAY	WEDNESDAY	THURSDAY	FRIDAY	SATURDAY
1	2	3	4	5	6 Waitangi Day (NZ)	7
8	9	10	11	12	13	14 St. Valentine's Day
15	16 Presidents' Day (USA)	17	18	19	20	21
22	23	24	25 Ash Wednesday	26	27	28

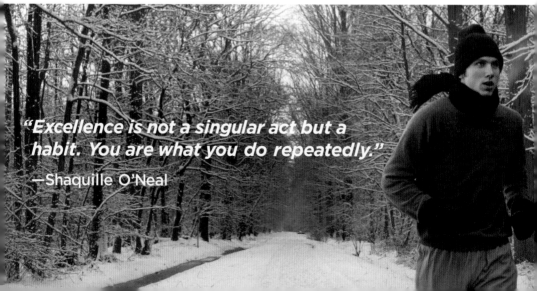

"*Excellence is not a singular act but a habit. You are what you do repeatedly.*"

—Shaquille O'Neal

HEART

A spike in marathon deaths over the past two years raises the question that has dogged running since it first burst into American popularity: Is it safe? No matter how ardently physicians and sports physiologists argue that you're more likely to die from *not* running, the risks are real. And the bets are being played out in the middle of your chest.

To be sure, bad judgments in hydration and heat also kill runners every year. But by far, the greatest risks are tied to your body's central pump. You can eliminate some of these risks outright; others you can hedge. And there are still others that simply won't bend to training and will. You'll have to adapt your goals and desires to their mortal constraints.

If you have a family history of heart disease, you need your doctor's blessing before you begin hard training. After 40, especially if you're male, an electrocardiogram, a blood test, and a treadmill stress test every two to three years will typically set you free. But if close relatives (your parents or a sibling) have heart disease, you should ask your doctor about a 64-slice CT scan. It's a new, noninvasive technology that takes finely layered, 3-D images of your heart. It alerts doctors to otherwise undetected blockages in arteries. Early studies show it to be stunningly accurate.

Good diet can also hedge the genetic odds stacked against you, especially high cholesterol. It can't reverse decades of bad habits, however, and its benefits accrue over years, not in the relatively short time it takes to train for a marathon or shed 10 pounds. The same is true of various heart remedies, over-the-counter and otherwise. Fish oil, niacin, low-dosage aspirin, statins, beta blockers, and ezetimibe can lower a runner's risks for heart attack and stroke. But they're not miracle cures. Runners too easily oversell themselves on the benefits of drugs and good nutrition. It's an extension of the exuberance we get from training. Running makes dramatic changes in our bodies and in the way we feel. We can't help but believe that drugs and diet deliver the same quick results. They don't, and to believe otherwise is to dance with the Grim Reaper.

In fact, consistency is the best friend a runner's heart can have— nowhere more so than in training itself. The episodic athlete who indulges months of sedentary living, but then begins training hard for a race runs a far greater risk of stroke or a heart attack than the runner who maintains at least a minimum level of aerobic fitness throughout the year. With age, the dangers of on-again, off-again training jump.

It's painful to face the limitations of your mortal body. It's equally important not to panic yourself from headlines. The number of recent marathon deaths has risen because the number of marathons and their runners continues to rise exponentially. Make no mistake, running is good for your heart. It's just that you have to use your head about it. ■

Distance carried forward:

2 Monday   33

Where & When: Distance:
Comments:

3 Tuesday   34

Where & When: Distance:
Comments:

4 Wednesday   35

Where & When: Distance:
Comments:

5 Thursday   36

Where & When: Distance:
Comments:

6 Friday   37

Where & When: Distance:
Comments:

February

Saturday **7**

Where & When: Distance:

Comments:

Sunday **8**

Where & When: Distance:

Comments:

© Christoph Gramann/zefa/CORBIS

tip: New running clothes are less likely to chafe if you run them through the washer first.

Distance this week: Weight:

Distance carried forward: _____

9 Monday 40

_____

_____

Where & When: _____ **Distance:** _____

Comments: _____

_____

10 Tuesday 41

_____

_____

Where & When: _____ **Distance:** _____

Comments: _____

_____

11 Wednesday 42

_____

_____

Where & When: _____ **Distance:** _____

Comments: _____

_____

12 Thursday 43

_____

_____

Where & When: _____ **Distance:** _____

Comments: _____

_____

13 Friday 44

_____

_____

Where & When: _____ **Distance:** _____

Comments: _____

_____

February

Saturday 14

Where & When: Distance:

Comments:

Sunday 15

Where & When: Distance:

Comments:

© Chase Jarvis/CORBIS

tip: Worried about blocked arteries? Ask your doctor to check your blood pressure from both arms. A difference of 20 to 40 mm HG could indicate blockage.

Distance this week: **Weight:**

16 Monday 47

Where & When: **Distance:**

Comments:

17 Tuesday 48

Where & When: **Distance:**

Comments:

18 Wednesday 49

Where & When: **Distance:**

Comments:

19 Thursday 50

Where & When: **Distance:**

Comments:

20 Friday 51

Where & When: **Distance:**

Comments:

February

52

Where & When: _____ Distance: _____

Comments: _____

53

Where & When: _____ Distance: _____

Comments: _____

© Rick Gomez/CORBIS

tip: Shed mittens or gloves as soon as hands are warm. Your palms vent heat. Covered hands may ultimately inhibit your endurance.

Distance this week: _____ **Weight:** _____

Distance carried forward:

23 Monday 54

Where & When: Distance:

Comments:

24 Tuesday 55

Where & When: Distance:

Comments:

25 Wednesday 56

Where & When: Distance:

Comments:

26 Thursday 57

Where & When: Distance:

Comments:

27 Friday 58

Where & When: Distance:

Comments:

59   Saturday **28**

Where & When: Distance:

Comments:

60   Sunday **1**

Where & When: Distance:

Comments:

tip:

Snowshoeing is an excellent alternative to your easy run. Use time on the snow, rather than mileage, to determine your workout.

tip: Ibuprofen may counteract aspirin's benefits to your heart. Talk to your doctor about which over-the-counter drug to use for muscle pain.

tip: Consistency in training—weekly mileage and accumulated years of running—is the decisive factor in preventing cardiovascular disease.

Notes:

Distance this week: Weight:

March

SUNDAY	MONDAY	TUESDAY	WEDNESDAY	THURSDAY	FRIDAY	SATURDAY
1 St. David's Day (UK)	2 Labour Day (Australia—WA)	3	4	5	6	7
8 International Women's Day	9 Eight Hours Day (Australia—TAS) Labour Day (Australia—VIC) Commonwealth Day (Australia, Canada, NZ, UK)	10 Purim	11	12	13	14
15	16 Canberra Day (Australia—ACT)	17 St. Patrick's Day	18	19	20	21
22 Mothering Sunday (UK)	23	24	25	26	27	28
29	30	31				

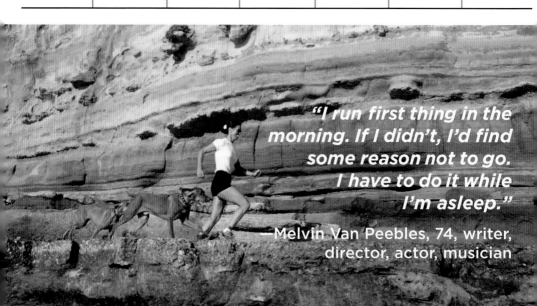

"I run first thing in the morning. If I didn't, I'd find some reason not to go. I have to do it while I'm asleep."

—Melvin Van Peebles, 74, writer, director, actor, musician

PARTNER

A dog brooks no excuses. Who cares that it's 35 degrees at daybreak with a downpour pelting the pavement? A cold nuzzle at your cheek says that it's time to get out of bed for your customary run.

This is only one reason that dogs better humans as running partners. You can't reason or beg your way out of a workout. A dog knows when you're shirking. Pleading eyes will follow you around the house like your mother's guilt. Worse, dogs will always hold up their end of the bargain. Unlike humans, they will never cancel, show up late, or beg to knock off early.

As athletes go, most dogs are superior to humans, certainly in speed. In all likelihood, your pup can beat the snot out of you. And yet better dogs obligingly run at your pace, along whatever course you decide—no whining, if trained right, and only the occasional urge to move things a little faster or to stray in pursuit of more interesting diversions, especially frightful, disgusting smells.

This brings up another advantage dogs have over humans: no talking. To be sure, many runners seek people partners for conversation. These relationships can be profoundly intimate, crucially supportive. Yet it's also true that when dialogue dominates a workout, either the intensity of the run or the depth of the conversation suffers. A dog will listen to your lust for a coworker, your mortal fear of circus clowns, or your secret desire to wear German lederhosen. The silent reply often lends perspective.

Even better, it refocuses your efforts on the workout at hand.

Dogs benefit from running, too, both physically and for their general spirits. Notice that when a dog gets to invent a game, especially with another pup, some form of chase will ensue. Instinct and exuberance drive this great enterprise. Dog trainers will tell you that many puppy problem behaviors—chewing furniture, whining, accidents on the rug—can be curbed with more exercise rather than with punishment or measures of control. This is especially true for dogs confined to small yards and cramped urban apartments. Daily, obligatory walks from time-pressed owners rarely do a pooch justice.

For workouts, dogs, like humans, gradually need to build distance. Respect the limits of ability—in the breed and also in the individual dog. Workouts on pavement shouldn't begin until the dog is nearly a year old. Be aware that heat stroke can kill a dog, even while your own body runs cool. If your terrier's tongue is dragging the ground, plan for water breaks and move your workouts to cooler parts of the day. Also be aware that dogs age more quickly than people and suffer many of the same afflictions: arthritis, osteoporosis, and general grumpiness.

In fact, accommodation is the key to making a dog a great running partner at any moment of your mutual lives. All those cold, rainy workout mornings will eventually remind you why you love your dog. They'll remind you why you love running. ■

Distance carried forward: _____

2 Monday 61

_____

Where & When: _____ **Distance:** _____
Comments: _____

_____

3 Tuesday 62

_____

Where & When: _____ **Distance:** _____
Comments: _____

_____

4 Wednesday 63

_____

Where & When: _____ **Distance:** _____
Comments: _____

_____

5 Thursday 64

_____

Where & When: _____ **Distance:** _____
Comments: _____

_____

6 Friday 65

_____

Where & When: _____ **Distance:** _____
Comments: _____

_____

March

Saturday **7**

Where & When: **Distance:**

Comments:

Sunday **8**

Where & When: **Distance:**

Comments:

© Anthony West/CORBIS

tip: The motivation, encouragement, and friendly competition from running with a group can do wonders for your performance.

Distance this week: **Weight:**

9 Monday 68

Where & When: **Distance:**

Comments:

10 Tuesday 69

Where & When: **Distance:**

Comments:

11 Wednesday 70

Where & When: **Distance:**

Comments:

12 Thursday 71

Where & When: **Distance:**

Comments:

13 Friday 72

Where & When: **Distance:**

Comments:

73

Saturday **14**

Where & When: Distance:

Comments:

74

Sunday **15**

Where & When: Distance:

Comments:

© CORBIS

tip: Does price tell you anything about the quality of a running shoe? No. A generation of sub-$40 shoes is beginning to challenge high-end brands. Let your feet decide.

Distance this week: **Weight:**

Distance carried forward:

16 Monday 75

Where & When: Distance:

Comments:

17 Tuesday 76

Where & When: Distance:

Comments:

18 Wednesday 77

Where & When: Distance:

Comments:

19 Thursday 78

Where & When: Distance:

Comments:

20 Friday 79

Where & When: Distance:

Comments:

March

Saturday **21**

Where & When: Distance:

Comments:

Sunday **22**

Where & When: Distance:

Comments:

© Karl Weatherly/CORBIS

tip: Most runners won't feel the effects of elevation on their performance unless they're running above 4,500 feet.

Distance this week: **Weight:**

Distance carried forward:

23 Monday   82

Where & When: Distance:
Comments:

24 Tuesday   83

Where & When: Distance:
Comments:

25 Wednesday   84

Where & When: Distance:
Comments:

26 Thursday   85

Where & When: Distance:
Comments:

27 Friday   86

Where & When: Distance:
Comments:

87 Saturday **28**

Where & When: Distance:

Comments:

88 Sunday **29**

Where & When: Distance:

Comments:

© CORBIS

tip: Long day ahead of you? Go for a run. You'll be more alert four to six hours afterward.

Distance this week: **Weight:**

Distance carried forward: _____

30 Monday 89
_____
_____

Where & When: _____ **Distance:** _____

Comments: _____
_____

31 Tuesday 90
_____
_____

Where & When: _____ **Distance:** _____

Comments: _____
_____

1 Wednesday 91
_____
_____

Where & When: _____ **Distance:** _____

Comments: _____
_____

2 Thursday 92
_____
_____

Where & When: _____ **Distance:** _____

Comments: _____
_____

3 Friday 93
_____
_____

Where & When: _____ **Distance:** _____

Comments: _____
_____

94   **Saturday 4**

Where & When: **Distance:**

Comments:

95   **Sunday 5**

Where & When: **Distance:**

Comments:

tip:

Hypothermia can strike on even mildly cool days, especially if it's raining. The signs to look for: shivering, weakness, lethargy, light-headedness, and mild confusion.

tip: Running has the same physiological effect as Valium for reducing anxiety and stress.

tip: Keep running clothes in your car. If traffic reports warn of a snarled commute, go for a run as you wait for congestion to clear.

Notes:

Distance this week: **Weight:**

April

SUNDAY	MONDAY	TUESDAY	WEDNESDAY	THURSDAY	FRIDAY	SATURDAY
			1	2	3	4
5 Palm Sunday	6	7	8	9 First day of Passover	10 Good Friday (Western)	11 Easter Saturday (Australia—except TAS, WA)
12 Easter (Western)	13 Easter Monday (Australia, Canada, NZ, UK—except Scotland)	14	15	16 Last day of Passover	17 Holy Friday (Orthodox)	18
19 Easter (Orthodox)	20	21	22 Earth Day	23 St. George's Day (UK)	24	25 Anzac Day (Australia, NZ)
26	27 Anzac Day (observed) (Australia—WA)	28	29	30		

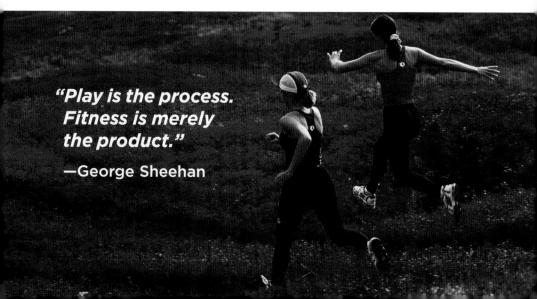

"Play is the process. Fitness is merely the product."
—George Sheehan

PLAY

We are first seduced into running as children, usually by the exuberance of speed. Then we get all rational and buttoned down about it. Too often speed becomes a mechanized subsidiary of our running programs —interval training for racers, and infrequent drills and hill charges for the rest of us. The joy of speed is driven from our workouts.

Pleasure aside, the payoff is sweet. We get progressively stronger with smaller amounts of effort. Sprinters have no alternative. Interval training—repetitive, calculated bursts of speed followed by ever-shorter recovery periods— is the single most powerful tool discovered in the past 70 years for improving performance. Middle distance runners benefit as well, since intervals improve stamina in the late stages of a race. And now even marathoners are discovering the sublime magic of intervals. Training hours can be slashed with no hit to performance. Intervals allow more time for rest between workouts, which is when muscle is built. They reduce the risk of injury. Two of the leading marathon programs in the country now try to eek out more speed and endurance with less training time. Intervals are key.

Noncompetitive runners, on the other hand, tend to eschew any form of speed work, except as diversion—to strengthen neglected muscles and to bring variation to the workout. Yet a tide of evidence shows that interval training benefits those trying to lose weight, pre-diabetics, beginners, runners over 65, those returning from knee and foot injuries, cross-trainers, those with irregular workout schedules, and trail runners. Intervals help you lose weight with less work. They dramatically improve the efficiency with which your body uses oxygen. They increase stamina and speed. And these benefits accrue quickly— often within a matter of weeks. Suddenly, runners can't run away from speed. No matter what your goals are, intervals will help you achieve them.

Of course, cod-liver oil and colonoscopies are good for you, too, though *pleasure* doesn't exactly capture their essence. So approach intervals as play. On your next run, simply put on a sprint. Enjoy it. When you begin to feel winded, slow to almost a jog. Once you recover, put on another sprint. This is your essential interval. How fast you go is less important than how long you sustain the quick pace. When the challenge and exuberance begin to please you, you'll want to use a stopwatch and, if you have one, a heart-rate monitor. There are all manner of interval workouts on the Internet; coaches and trainers perfect and post their techniques as if they were alchemy.

Play should continue to guide you, even if you're a competitive runner. There are very few other rules that matter. Don't do intervals on successive workouts. Give yourself a longer cool-down session before you stop. If you've had a serious leg injury, if you have a heart condition, or if you're over 50 years old, talk to your doctor first. Otherwise, return to speed work with a child's point of view. ■

Distance carried forward: _____

6 Monday 96
_____

Where & When: _____ **Distance:** _____
Comments: _____
_____

7 Tuesday 97
_____

Where & When: _____ **Distance:** _____
Comments: _____
_____

8 Wednesday 98
_____

Where & When: _____ **Distance:** _____
Comments: _____
_____

9 Thursday 99
_____

Where & When: _____ **Distance:** _____
Comments: _____
_____

10 Friday 100
_____

Where & When: _____ **Distance:** _____
Comments: _____
_____

April

Saturday 11

Where & When: **Distance:**

Comments:

Sunday 12

Where & When: **Distance:**

Comments:

© Tim Tadder/CORBIS

tip: It's rare to develop allergies after your late 20s or early 30s. If you're suddenly afflicted with congestion, eye irritation, or a runny nose, talk to your doctor.

Distance this week: **Weight:**

Distance carried forward: _____

13 Monday   103
_____

_____

Where & When: _____   **Distance:** _____
Comments: _____

_____

14 Tuesday   104
_____

_____

Where & When: _____   **Distance:** _____
Comments: _____

_____

15 Wednesday   105
_____

_____

Where & When: _____   **Distance:** _____
Comments: _____

_____

16 Thursday   106
_____

_____

Where & When: _____   **Distance:** _____
Comments: _____

_____

17 Friday   107
_____

_____

Where & When: _____   **Distance:** _____
Comments: _____

_____

April

Where & When: **Distance:**

Comments:

Where & When: **Distance:**

Comments:

© Larry Williams/CORBIS

tip: Don't over-taper your workouts before a big race. Drop to 90 percent of your peak workout three weeks from the race date, to 75 percent at two weeks, and to 65 percent the week before.

Distance this week: **Weight:**

Distance carried forward:

20 Monday   110

Where & When: **Distance:**
Comments:

21 Tuesday   111

Where & When: **Distance:**
Comments:

22 Wednesday   112

Where & When: **Distance:**
Comments:

23 Thursday   113

Where & When: **Distance:**
Comments:

24 Friday   114

Where & When: **Distance:**
Comments:

115   Saturday **25**

Where & When: Distance:

Comments:

116   Sunday **26**

Where & When: Distance:

Comments:

© Randy Faris/CORBIS

tip: If you spend the winter running on a treadmill or a track, slowly alternate these with road runs during the spring until your body becomes accustomed to the harder surfaces.

Distance this week: Weight:

Distance carried forward: _____

27 Monday   117
_____

Where & When: _____ **Distance:** _____
Comments: _____
_____

28 Tuesday   118
_____

Where & When: _____ **Distance:** _____
Comments: _____
_____

29 Wednesday   119
_____

Where & When: _____ **Distance:** _____
Comments: _____
_____

30 Thursday   120
_____

Where & When: _____ **Distance:** _____
Comments: _____
_____

1 Friday   121
_____

Where & When: _____ **Distance:** _____
Comments: _____
_____

122   Saturday **2**

Where & When: Distance:
Comments:

123   Sunday **3**

Where & When: Distance:
Comments:

tip:

Don't bob and weave your way through the starting pack of a race. You'll just squander energy.

tip: In the early months of a healthy pregnancy, running is safe and beneficial.

tip: When passing a rival in a race, move quickly. It suggests you feel better than you probably do.

Notes:

Distance this week: Weight:

May

SUNDAY	MONDAY	TUESDAY	WEDNESDAY	THURSDAY	FRIDAY	SATURDAY
					1	2
3	4 Labour Day (Australia—QLD) Early May Bank Holiday (Eire, UK, Australia—NT)	5	6	7	8	9
10 Mother's Day (USA, Australia, Canada, NZ)	11	12	13	14	15	16 Armed Forces Day (USA)
17	18 Victoria Day (Canada)	19	20	21	22	23
24 / 31	25 Memorial Day (USA) Spring Bank Holiday (UK)	26	27	28	29	30

"We run to undo the damage we've done to body and spirit. We run to find some part of ourselves undiscovered."

—John "The Penguin" Bingham, columnist, *Runner's World*

FEET

Make amends to your feet. They have been neglected, downright ignored. You entomb them in expensive, highly cushioned running shoes as if to shut them up. And yet injuries related to your knees, hips, and lower back can often be traced to your feet. With each step they catch several times your weight on landing and then fluidly and gracefully launch you into the next step.

This movement—innate, complex—puts stress on many parts of your trotters. After all, one-fourth of your body's bones are in your feet. The hoists and ligaments that convey a runner down the uncertain path are subject to overuse injuries, especially the dreaded duo of *itises:* plantar fasciitis and Achilles tendonitis. The former afflicts the thick band of tissue that stretches from toes to heel and is prone to tearing with overuse, resulting in inflammation (and fiery pain) at the heel. The Achilles tendon is the largest, thickest tendon in your body, running from your heel to your calf. When the sheath surrounding it becomes inflamed from overuse, it results in sharp pain in the narrow band of tissue at the back of your ankle. Quite often, it appears early in a workout, disappears, and then returns.

A high weekly mileage is less likely to provoke overuse injuries than the accumulated demands within a workout: hill charges, interval training, or dramatic changes in terrain. If the pain is sporadic and acute, the remedy is to dramatically scale back your workouts. Lie low for several weeks before you gradually begin pushing again. If the pain is chronic, the remedy is to stop running. This is a shocker, of course, and the news gets worse: chronic overuse injuries take months, not weeks, to heal. A single workout can provoke the old demon in all its fury. During recovery, you'll want to switch to elliptical trainers, swimming, bicycling—anything except running.

Aside from overuse injuries, your feet can aggravate myriad other types of pains throughout your body. When isolating the source, begin with your shoes. Perhaps it's time to try not only a new pair, but a new shoe store as well. Shop in the afternoon when your feet are fully engorged. Solicit the help of a salesperson who runs (a quick glance at his or her physique will tip you off). And mark down the date you buy your new pair in this log. Running shoes are only good for about 200 miles. Calculate accordingly.

Foot strength and balance exercises can eliminate all manner of pain in your workouts as well. There are dozens of them: pick up marbles or pencils with your toes, do multiple sets of walking down a staircase backward, run barefoot along a sand dune or a beach (trail running is good, too, but use shoes), put light weights on the tops of your feet and lift them, balance on one foot while standing on a mini-trampoline or a wobble board, and so forth. Almost any exertion that works the supporting muscles in your feet can ease pain. Remember that the stronger the foot, the stronger the runner. ■

Distance carried forward:

4 Monday   124

Where & When: **Distance:**

Comments:

5 Tuesday   125

Where & When: **Distance:**

Comments:

6 Wednesday   126

Where & When: **Distance:**

Comments:

7 Thursday   127

Where & When: **Distance:**

Comments:

8 Friday   128

Where & When: **Distance:**

Comments:

May

Saturday **9**

Where & When: Distance:

Comments:

Sunday **10**

Where & When: Distance:

Comments:

© DiMaggio/Kalish/CORBIS

tip: Tie your shoes loosely before a marathon. Your feet will swell through the race; tight shoes can cause pain and blisters.

Distance this week: **Weight:**

Distance carried forward:

11 Monday 131

Where & When: Distance:

Comments:

12 Tuesday 132

Where & When: Distance:

Comments:

13 Wednesday 133

Where & When: Distance:

Comments:

14 Thursday 134

Where & When: Distance:

Comments:

15 Friday 135

Where & When: Distance:

Comments:

136 _____ Saturday **16**

_____

Where & When: _____ **Distance:** _____

Comments: _____

_____

137 _____ Sunday **17**

_____

Where & When: _____ **Distance:** _____

Comments: _____

_____

© Tim Tadder/CORBIS

tip: Hills are speed work in disguise. Be aware, however, that steep hills can aggravate the Achilles tendon and plantar fascia.

Distance this week: _____ **Weight:** _____

Distance carried forward:

18 Monday   138

Where & When: **Distance:**

Comments:

19 Tuesday   139

Where & When: **Distance:**

Comments:

20 Wednesday   140

Where & When: **Distance:**

Comments:

21 Thursday   141

Where & When: **Distance:**

Comments:

22 Friday   142

Where & When: **Distance:**

Comments:

May

Saturday **23**

Where & When: Distance:

Comments:

Sunday **24**

Where & When: Distance:

Comments:

© Steve Craft/CORBIS

tip: Training for your first marathon? Plan on running a half marathon at least one month before (even if you're the only participant). It provides a crucial reality check for pace and endurance.

Distance this week: Weight:

Distance carried forward: _____

25 Monday   145
_____
_____

Where & When: _____ **Distance:** _____
Comments: _____
_____

26 Tuesday   146
_____
_____

Where & When: _____ **Distance:** _____
Comments: _____
_____

27 Wednesday   147
_____
_____

Where & When: _____ **Distance:** _____
Comments: _____
_____

28 Thursday   148
_____
_____

Where & When: _____ **Distance:** _____
Comments: _____
_____

29 Friday   149
_____
_____

Where & When: _____ **Distance:** _____
Comments: _____
_____

150 Saturday **30**

Where & When: Distance:
Comments:

151 Sunday **31**

Where & When: Distance:
Comments:

tip:

When traveling to a race by air, wear your running shoes on the flight. They're the last thing you want the airline to lose.

tip: Once a child begins any form of structured workout, he or she should be fitted for running shoes.

tip: Plantar fasciitis, the most common form of heel pain, usually abates after a year, even if untreated.

Notes:

Distance this week: Weight:

June

SUNDAY	MONDAY	TUESDAY	WEDNESDAY	THURSDAY	FRIDAY	SATURDAY
	1 Queen's Birthday (NZ) Foundation Day (Australia—WA) Bank Holiday (Eire)	**2**	**3**	**4**	**5**	**6**
7	**8** Queen's Birthday (Australia—except WA)	**9**	**10**	**11**	**12**	**13**
14 Flag Day (USA)	**15**	**16**	**17**	**18**	**19**	**20**
21 Father's Day (USA, Canada, UK)	**22**	**23**	**24**	**25**	**26**	**27**
28	**29**	**30**				

"Life is a near-death experience."

—George Carlin

JUICED

You are a science project. With every workout, you focus calculated efforts on improving your body, with the results revealed in the next workout, the next race. In all likelihood, running describes not just something you do, but someone you are. And for this reason, scientific experimentation carries on well after you've shed your running shoes for the day—in your diet, for example.

Runners seize on food crazes with the same blind enthusiasm as anyone else and typically get the same disenchanting results. Yet how else do we learn? Carbohydrate loading before a distance race or workout undoubtedly forestalls bonking. Salty foods have long been proven to slow dehydration in hot weather. And no one needs to tell you that as your weekly mileage increases, so do your caloric needs. Hunger confronts a runner like a demanding but familiar dragon. It should remind you of the efficiency with which you burn fuel. It's okay to feed the dragon.

So when does experimentation go too far? The human body suffers dietary nostrums with surprising forgiveness. Frankly, it's astonishing how we survive what we eat. It's likewise surprising how little it matters in athletic performance. Kenyan marathoners may have many secrets for why they consistently win, but their breakfasts won't reveal much. Over months and years we want to develop eating habits that better our abilities while also extending our lives. Unfortunately, no single regimen prevails. The best advice that nutritionists and sports physiologists collectively purvey is to eat a varied and balanced diet.

Most of us don't consume enough fruits and vegetables. So eat your broccoli.

With so little specific advice available, many runners experiment with the exploding stable of dietary supplements, some of which were purportedly formulated with running in mind. Approach these with skepticism. Only four supplements have demonstrated unqualified effectiveness by the National Institutes of Health: vitamin D and calcium for women at risk of osteoporosis, folate for pregnant women, and fish oil (with omega-3 fatty acids) for lowering cholesterol and blood pressure. Everything else is taken on faith—or because of the results you're actually getting. But bear in mind that the Food and Drug Administration has very little authority over the $21 billion supplements industry. Charlatans and snake-oil salesman are rife.

Food crazes of any kind seduce runners with the same promise of training itself: a calculated, marginal benefit. Your bases are covered. Or perhaps it's just easier to buy something than to change something. Truth is, adding hill charges to your workouts or grabbing an extra hour of sleep will often do more for your performance than timing your protein intake or popping a magic pill. The key is to be aware when you're getting carried away with a dietary idea.

In the meantime, be grateful for the ferocity of appetite that running brings. It's no secret that runners live life more fully than sedentary people. Hunger should be a vibrant signal of how rich your experience has become. ■

Distance carried forward:

1 Monday 152

Where & When: Distance:
Comments:

2 Tuesday 153

Where & When: Distance:
Comments:

3 Wednesday 154

Where & When: Distance:
Comments:

4 Thursday 155

Where & When: Distance:
Comments:

5 Friday 156

Where & When: Distance:
Comments:

June

Saturday **6**

Where & When: **Distance:**

Comments:

Sunday **7**

Where & When: **Distance:**

Comments:

© Duomo/CORBIS

tip: Rotating running shoes lets each pair thoroughly dry out. They'll also last longer.

Distance this week: **Weight:**

Distance carried forward: _____

8 Monday 159
_____

Where & When: _____ **Distance:** _____
Comments: _____
_____

9 Tuesday 160
_____

Where & When: _____ **Distance:** _____
Comments: _____
_____

10 Wednesday 161
_____

Where & When: _____ **Distance:** _____
Comments: _____
_____

11 Thursday 162
_____

Where & When: _____ **Distance:** _____
Comments: _____
_____

12 Friday 163
_____

Where & When: _____ **Distance:** _____
Comments: _____
_____

June

Saturday 13

Where & When: **Distance:**

Comments:

Sunday 14

Where & When: **Distance:**

Comments:

© Steve Prezant/CORBIS

tip: There is absolutely no evidence that protein supplements improve your endurance, speed, or recovery times.

Distance this week: **Weight:**

Distance carried forward:

15 Monday 166

Where & When: Distance:

Comments:

16 Tuesday 167

Where & When: Distance:

Comments:

17 Wednesday 168

Where & When: Distance:

Comments:

18 Thursday 169

Where & When: Distance:

Comments:

19 Friday 170

Where & When: Distance:

Comments:

June

171   **Saturday 20**

Where & When: **Distance:**

Comments:

172   **Sunday 21**

Where & When: **Distance:**

Comments:

© Chase Jarvis/CORBIS

tip: Most people don't slather on sufficient sunscreen for protection against UVA rays, the primary source of skin cancer. Pour it on thick, never mind the ghost-like pallor it gives you.

Distance this week: **Weight:**

Distance carried forward:

22 Monday 173

Where & When: **Distance:**

Comments:

23 Tuesday 174

Where & When: **Distance:**

Comments:

24 Wednesday 175

Where & When: **Distance:**

Comments:

25 Thursday 176

Where & When: **Distance:**

Comments:

26 Friday 177

Where & When: **Distance:**

Comments:

June

Saturday 27

Where & When: Distance:

Comments:

Sunday 28

Where & When: Distance:

Comments:

© Gareth Brown/CORBIS

tip: Running shoes with narrow heels improve rear-foot control and reduce injuries to your lower extremities.

Distance this week: Weight:

29 Monday   180

Where & When: **Distance:**

Comments:

30 Tuesday   181

Where & When: **Distance:**

Comments:

1 Wednesday   182

Where & When: **Distance:**

Comments:

2 Thursday   183

Where & When: **Distance:**

Comments:

3 Friday   184

Where & When: **Distance:**

Comments:

June/July

185 Saturday **4**

Where & When: Distance:

Comments:

186 Sunday **5**

Where & When: Distance:

Comments:

tip:

In a triathlon, begin hydrating as soon as you finish the swimming leg—the earlier the better. In all likelihood, your closing run will be faster.

tip: The best energy bars combine fruit, whole grains, and a soluble form of fiber. Total carbohydrates should be at least 40 grams.

tip: Eat as soon as you can after a workout. You'll recover faster.

Notes:

Distance this week: Weight:

July

SUNDAY	MONDAY	TUESDAY	WEDNESDAY	THURSDAY	FRIDAY	SATURDAY
			1 Canada Day	2	3	4 Independence Day (USA)
5	6	7	8	9	10	11
12	13	14	15	16	17	18
19	20	21	22	23	24	25
26	27	28	29	30	31	

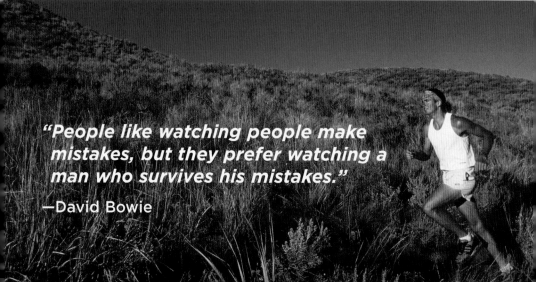

"People like watching people make mistakes, but they prefer watching a man who survives his mistakes."

—David Bowie

FIRE

Who can blame Icarus for flying too close to the sun? Every runner has known the rapture from flight that casts caution aside. And many of us have likewise had our wings melted from the heat. We tend to be shortsighted about the perils of hot-weather months, taking precautions only for a single day's workout or race. Like Icarus, what we really need is a long-range flight plan.

When the days begin to bake, you'll have to adapt your workouts not only to heat, but to humidity. The body cools with the evaporation of sweat. In high humidity, sweat doesn't evaporate; it cocoons you in your own lovely slime. And until you acclimate, you'll have to slow your pace for both short and long distances. From the onset of sticky weather, plan to give yourself two weeks in which all measures of speed are laid aside. Incidentally, you'll hasten your acclimation by spending non-workout time outdoors as well—puttering in the yard, walking, and any kind of low-intensity activity.

Old habits might also have to be put aside for the summer. Your customary after-work run might wisely be swapped for a pre-dawn workout, when the air is cleanest and temperatures allow for longer distances. If possible, cross train indoors during the hot months. Run intervals and speed work on a treadmill. And be willing to postpone summer races for cooler months.

If you run before dawn, you'll need reflective clothes and possibly a headlamp or lightweight handheld flashlight that let you alert oncoming traffic. Consider adding to your other gear as well. Hats with broad brims are a must (mesh caps, in particular, release heat but shield you from sun rays). Loose fitting long-sleeved shirts with wicking abilities fend off the sun from bare skin. The same is true of longer, baggy running shorts. Sports sunglasses—the American Optometric Association recommends specs that block 99 to 100 percent of UVA rays—also protect your eyes from gravel kicked up by passing cars. Likewise, use broad-spectrum sunscreen, which protects against both UVA and UVB rays. Slather it on thick.

Hydration presents a too-little, too-much quandary. The most accurate way to find out how much water you need is to weigh yourself in the buff before, and then immediately after, your customary long run. Every pound lost amounts to about 16 ounces of fluid. Drink at least this much an hour before your workout. With high humidity or speed work, you'll need more. If you simply don't know how long you'll be running, try to drink between 14 and 27 ounces per hour. And make sure you have water stops planned along your route.

Finally, be resourceful. If you're running under a humid cloud cover, dress so that you can strip off as much clothing as possible without fetching attention from the police. A sponge under your hat with ice cubes fitted atop will keep your head cool. Likewise, ice cubes wrapped in a bandana and tied around your neck can do wonders. ∎

Distance carried forward: _____

6 Monday 187
_____

Where & When: _____ **Distance:** _____
Comments: _____
_____

7 Tuesday 188
_____

Where & When: _____ **Distance:** _____
Comments: _____
_____

8 Wednesday 189
_____

Where & When: _____ **Distance:** _____
Comments: _____
_____

9 Thursday 190
_____

Where & When: _____ **Distance:** _____
Comments: _____
_____

10 Friday 191
_____

Where & When: _____ **Distance:** _____
Comments: _____
_____

July

Saturday 11

Where & When: Distance:

Comments:

Sunday 12

Where & When: Distance:

Comments:

© David Vintiner/zefa/CORBIS

tip: Cold drinks during and after a run not only help cool your body, but they empty from the stomach faster than hot beverages, helping you rehydrate more quickly.

Distance this week: **Weight:**

Distance carried forward: _____

13 Monday 194
_____

Where & When: _____ **Distance:** _____
Comments: _____
_____

14 Tuesday 195
_____

Where & When: _____ **Distance:** _____
Comments: _____
_____

15 Wednesday 196
_____

Where & When: _____ **Distance:** _____
Comments: _____
_____

16 Thursday 197
_____

Where & When: _____ **Distance:** _____
Comments: _____
_____

17 Friday 198
_____

Where & When: _____ **Distance:** _____
Comments: _____
_____

July

Saturday 18

Where & When: **Distance:**

Comments:

Sunday 19

Where & When: **Distance:**

Comments:

© Chase Jarvis/CORBIS

tip: Don't ignore the signs of fatigue: a burning sensation in the legs or a pounding and rapid heart rate that doesn't slow even when you rest. These tell you it's time to knock off for the day.

Distance this week: **Weight:**

Distance carried forward:

20 Monday 201

Where & When: Distance:

Comments:

21 Tuesday 202

Where & When: Distance:

Comments:

22 Wednesday 203

Where & When: Distance:

Comments:

23 Thursday 204

Where & When: Distance:

Comments:

24 Friday 205

Where & When: Distance:

Comments:

July

Saturday 25

Where & When: **Distance:**

Comments:

Sunday 26

Where & When: **Distance:**

Comments:

© CORBIS

tip: Racing courtesy: run in a straight line whenever possible.
Look before you veer, spit, or blow your nose. And don't dodge
in front of another runner until you're at least two steps ahead.

Distance this week: **Weight:**

Distance carried forward:

27 Monday   208

Where & When: Distance:

Comments:

28 Tuesday   209

Where & When: Distance:

Comments:

29 Wednesday   210

Where & When: Distance:

Comments:

30 Thursday   211

Where & When: Distance:

Comments:

31 Friday   212

Where & When: Distance:

Comments:

213 _____ **Saturday 1**

_____

Where & When: _____ **Distance:** _____

Comments: _____

_____

214 _____ **Sunday 2**

_____

Where & When: _____ **Distance:** _____

Comments: _____

_____

tip:

Cotton hates humidity. It will weigh you down, chafe, and trap heat. If you've resisted running clothes with wicking properties, humid days should change your mind.

tip: For workouts lasting more than an hour and a half, switch from water to a high-sodium sports drink, which will replenish fluids faster.

tip: Early morning runners suffer more injuries than afternoon runners, so take extra care.

Notes: _____

_____

_____

Distance this week: _____ **Weight:** _____

August

SUNDAY	MONDAY	TUESDAY	WEDNESDAY	THURSDAY	FRIDAY	SATURDAY
						1
2	3 Bank Holiday (Eire, Scotland, Australia—ACT, NSW) Picnic Day (Australia—NT)	4	5	6	7	8
9	10	11	12	13	14	15
16	17	18	19	20	21	22
23	24	25	26	27	28	29
30	31 Summer Bank Holiday (UK—except Scotland)					

"It's easy to have faith in yourself and have discipline when you're a winner—when you're number one. What you got to have is faith and discipline when you're not a winner."

—Vince Lombardi

PERSISTENCE

Non-runners marvel at the discipline of runners, even though it's mistaken awe. Sure, discipline is required to get any training program going. And often it's the only thing that will jimmy us out the door when it's wet and freezing, when we're pressed for time, or when we're distracted by the diverse demands of daily living. But early in any workout program, discipline gracefully bows away to plain old persistence, which is the more powerful motivator. Every workout brings results, and so we want more. We yearn to stick with it.

Persistence pays, to be sure, but it can also waver, especially when the bounty of early benefits from training starts to ebb. This presents a great time to reassess your goals. You can shave minutes off your mile in the months when you're new to running. But once you're logging a steady 20 miles a week or more, you'll be able to shed only seconds, at best. This doesn't require you to lower your expectations. It means that you'll have to become more specific in your goals, more attuned to subtler advances in performance. The same is true of distance goals. Though you can certainly add miles to your weekly long run, you can't double your distance every ten weeks forever.

Another way that persistence can let you down is when it leads you into trouble. Sometimes it's wise to simply abandon a goal—or change it. We often don't recognize this until a tide of evidence has washed over us. Training brings such steadfast and predictable results that it's easy to believe that any goal is within reach if you just keep working at it. Worse, when desired results fail to materialize, you may find yourself pushing harder than you should, risking injury. It's hard for anyone to face personal limitations, especially when every workout brings some form of improvement, even if it isn't the kind you seek. But running reveals essential truths about who we are. If persistence in your training isn't bringing you closer to your goal, it's time to change the goal.

Besides, changing it is much less painful that failing at it. It's less painful than nursing an injury provoked by dogged pursuit of an elusive ideal. Both of these calamities can kill any form of motivation outright.

The best way to avoid this fate is to be greedy for information in your workouts—collecting not only the times and distances you log in these pages, but weather, road conditions, your mood, and level of perceived effort. Stay dialed in to how your body is performing and why. Elite runners don't dissociate. Mid-pack runners, on the other hand, tend to let their minds run to anything other than the discomfort and exhaustion they feel from their struggling bodies. Go ahead and feel the pain. Use it. Analyze it as best you can to refocus and hone your training program. It is the cornerstone to becoming a better runner. It helps persistence persist. ∎

Distance carried forward: _____

3 Monday   215

_____

Where & When: _____ **Distance:** _____

Comments: _____

_____

4 Tuesday   216

_____

Where & When: _____ **Distance:** _____

Comments: _____

_____

5 Wednesday   217

_____

Where & When: _____ **Distance:** _____

Comments: _____

_____

6 Thursday   218

_____

Where & When: _____ **Distance:** _____

Comments: _____

_____

7 Friday   219

_____

Where & When: _____ **Distance:** _____

Comments: _____

_____

August

Saturday **8**

Where & When: | **Distance:**

Comments:

Sunday **9**

Where & When: | **Distance:**

Comments:

© Timothy Tadder/CORBIS

tip: If your quadriceps (the muscles just north of your knees) hurt when you descend stairs or a hill after a hard race or workout, you may have damaged them. Try descending stairs backward until you're fully healed.

Distance this week: | **Weight:**

Distance carried forward:

10 Monday   222

Where & When: **Distance:**

Comments:

11 Tuesday   223

Where & When: **Distance:**

Comments:

12 Wednesday   224

Where & When: **Distance:**

Comments:

13 Thursday   225

Where & When: **Distance:**

Comments:

14 Friday   226

Where & When: **Distance:**

Comments:

227

Where & When: **Distance:**

Comments:

228

Where & When: **Distance:**

Comments:

© CORBIS

tip: Running on concrete is much harder on knees, ankles, and feet than running on asphalt.

Distance this week: **Weight:**

Distance carried forward:

17 Monday   229

Where & When: **Distance:**

Comments:

18 Tuesday   230

Where & When: **Distance:**

Comments:

19 Wednesday   231

Where & When: **Distance:**

Comments:

20 Thursday   232

Where & When: **Distance:**

Comments:

21 Friday   233

Where & When: **Distance:**

Comments:

234

Saturday **22**

Where & When: **Distance:**

Comments:

235

Sunday **23**

Where & When: **Distance:**

Comments:

© Tim Tadder/CORBIS

tip: When returning from an injury, plan about two weeks of retraining for every week you were sidelined to reach your previous performance.

Distance this week: **Weight:**

Distance carried forward:

24 Monday   236

Where & When: Distance:

Comments:

25 Tuesday   237

Where & When: Distance:

Comments:

26 Wednesday   238

Where & When: Distance:

Comments:

27 Thursday   239

Where & When: Distance:

Comments:

28 Friday   240

Where & When: Distance:

Comments:

August

Saturday 29

Where & When: **Distance:**

Comments:

Sunday 30

Where & When: **Distance:**

Comments:

© Anthony West/CORBIS

tip: Running in sand increases the intensity of your workout by as much as 20 percent—and builds proprioceptor muscles as well.

Distance this week: **Weight:**

Distance carried forward:

31 Monday   243

Where & When: **Distance:**
Comments:

1 Tuesday   244

Where & When: **Distance:**
Comments:

2 Wednesday   245

Where & When: **Distance:**
Comments:

3 Thursday   246

Where & When: **Distance:**
Comments:

4 Friday   247

Where & When: **Distance:**
Comments:

Aug/Sept

Saturday **5**

Where & When: Distance:

Comments:

Sunday **6**

Where & When: Distance:

Comments:

tip:

Intermittent icing—ice for ten minutes, off for ten minutes—works better at reducing swelling and pain than twenty minutes of steady icing.

tip: When descending a hill, drop your center of gravity by bending your knees a little. You'll conserve energy and maintain your balance.

tip: Hot weather is great for trail running. Not only does the canopy of trees deflect heat overhead, but grassy surfaces reflect less heat than concrete and asphalt.

Notes:

Distance this week: Weight:

September

SUNDAY	MONDAY	TUESDAY	WEDNESDAY	THURSDAY	FRIDAY	SATURDAY
		1	2	3	4	5
6 Father's Day (Australia, NZ)	7 Labor Day (USA, Canada)	8	9	10	11	12
13	14	15	16	17	18	19 Rosh Hashanah begins
20 Rosh Hashanah ends	21 U.N. International Day of Peace	22	23	24	25	26
27	28 Yom Kippur Queen's Birthday (Australia—WA)	29	30			

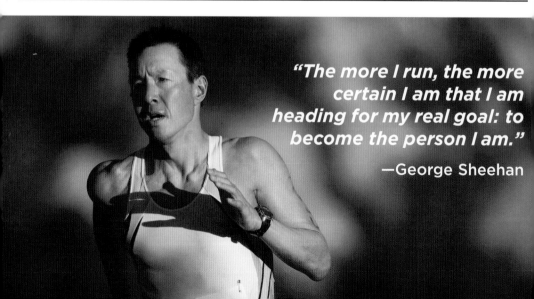

"The more I run, the more certain I am that I am heading for my real goal: to become the person I am."

—George Sheehan

HUMILITY

No one masters the marathon. No one conquers the mile. World records stand only to fall. And sooner or later your own personal best time will stubbornly refuse to be bested. These are the cruel stakes of competitive running, and any training program that fails to acknowledge them is doomed.

Still, they shouldn't discourage you—quite the opposite. The uncertainty of outcome is racing's greatest appeal. Planned effort, determination, and buckets of sweat will get you to the starting line. But then you have to relinquish control. The drama that unfolds reveals essential truths about your abilities and about your character. You can't possibly know these until the starting gun pops. Best of all, every race is a new opportunity to find these truths.

One secret to competitive running is to eliminate, as far as possible, the variables that would prevent you from performing at your best. This sounds obvious, but it works in subtle ways. You should anticipate specific challenges in the course, the weather, the size of the starting pack, and anything else that's going to affect your day. Likewise, racing too little or too much before your target event can undermine your efforts. Rehearsal races dispel jitters, help you establish pacing, and accustom you to packs of runners, drinking on the run, and other details that play a bigger role than you might imagine. But if you crowd your calendar with these events, your program loses focus. You steal training time from your ultimate goal.

Another secret: freak out early. Elite runners plan their training schedules backward from race day. Many months before your target event you'll see the biggest gains in performance or endurance. You'll also see the staggering amount of work required to meet your goal— that is, if it's a good goal. This is the time to revise your training program or revise your race date. The longer you wait, the more likely you are to fail. Worse, the psychological setback from scotching a race three weeks prior brings up entirely different feelings of failure. Remember that every workout produces new information about your abilities. Act on it early.

Once you've locked into a program that's producing results, however, don't second-guess yourself. By race date, the consistency of your progress will matter more than the fine-tuning of work-outs or the sporadic conversion experiences you've had with odd drills or interval routines. And cramming certainly doesn't work; you only risk injury. If you feel that you're coming to an event less than ready, just remember that competition has the miraculous power to draw more from a runner than the runner knew was there.

Finally, be prepared for two rough patches in your event—even if it's a sprint. It's psychologically easy to overcome the first. The second will test your character. No matter how much you prepare for competition, fate invariably throws up cruel ambushes. Be willing to collect yourself with dignity and dust off. This is a victory in its own right, even if your ultimate goal slips away. The opportunity to vindicate it waits for you at your next race. ∎

Distance carried forward:

7 Monday 250

Where & When: **Distance:**

Comments:

8 Tuesday 251

Where & When: **Distance:**

Comments:

9 Wednesday 252

Where & When: **Distance:**

Comments:

10 Thursday 253

Where & When: **Distance:**

Comments:

11 Friday 254

Where & When: **Distance:**

Comments:

September

Saturday 12

Where & When: **Distance:**

Comments:

Sunday 13

Where & When: **Distance:**

Comments:

© Tim Tadder/CORBIS

tip: Don't be afraid to draft behind a runner working at your pace. It's not illegal or rude. In fact, it's just plain smart.

Distance this week: **Weight:**

Distance carried forward:

14 Monday   257

Where & When: **Distance:**

Comments:

15 Tuesday   258

Where & When: **Distance:**

Comments:

16 Wednesday   259

Where & When: **Distance:**

Comments:

17 Thursday   260

Where & When: **Distance:**

Comments:

18 Friday   261

Where & When: **Distance:**

Comments:

September

Saturday **19**

Where & When: Distance:

Comments:

Sunday **20**

Where & When: Distance:

Comments:

© Chase Jarvis/CORBIS

tip: Trail runners beware: snakes can bite even when they're dead and even when they're decapitated! Of 34 people hospitalized for snake bite in Arizona recently, four were struck by presumably dead snakes and two were bitten by a head with no body.

Distance this week: **Weight:**

Distance carried forward:

21 Monday 264

Where & When: Distance:

Comments:

22 Tuesday 265

Where & When: Distance:

Comments:

23 Wednesday 266

Where & When: Distance:

Comments:

24 Thursday 267

Where & When: Distance:

Comments:

25 Friday 268

Where & When: Distance:

Comments:

September

Saturday 26

Where & When: Distance:

Comments:

Sunday 27

Where & When: Distance:

Comments:

© Ted Levine/zefa/CORBIS

tip: Keep easy days easy. You should be able to speak in complete sentences while you run without gasping for breath. Your heart rate should not exceed 70 percent of its maximum.

Distance this week: Weight:

Distance carried forward:

28 Monday 271

Where & When: **Distance:**

Comments:

29 Tuesday 272

Where & When: **Distance:**

Comments:

30 Wednesday 273

Where & When: **Distance:**

Comments:

1 Thursday 274

Where & When: **Distance:**

Comments:

2 Friday 275

Where & When: **Distance:**

Comments:

276   **Saturday 3**

Where & When: _____ Distance: _____

Comments: _____

277   **Sunday 4**

Where & When: _____ Distance: _____

Comments: _____

tip:

You should go into any race with a range of goals. These not only enhance your odds for success, but they hedge against countless variables that are beyond your control.

tip: On race day, pin a ten dollar bill on the underside of your singlet for emergencies.

tip: Believe it or not, an ultradistance race—100 miles or more—can be less stressful than a marathon because of the slower pace.

Notes: _____

_____

_____

Distance this week: _____   Weight: _____

October

SUNDAY	MONDAY	TUESDAY	WEDNESDAY	THURSDAY	FRIDAY	SATURDAY
				1	2	3
4	5 Labour Day (Australia—ACT, NSW, SA)	6	7	8	9	10
11	12 Columbus Day (USA) Thanksgiving (Canada)	13	14	15	16	17
18	19	20	21	22	23	24 United Nations Day
25	26 Labour Day (NZ) Bank Holiday (Eire)	27	28	29	30	31 Halloween

"When I'm doing hills, I say to myself, I love the hill, I love the hill. It helps."

—Shawn Colvin, singer-songwriter

FORM

You were probably surprised the first time you saw a videotape of yourself running or glimpsed your bobbing form in the mirror while on a treadmill. The image you cut likely defied the ways you imagined your foot to drop, the poise of your launch, the ways your shoulders heaved with the weight of each step. Some runners are downright furious with the careening, bounding clown act they see. Yet they may be excellent runners. Will changes to your form make you faster or stronger?

In all likelihood, no. Track coaches have tinkered with their athletes' running forms for decades—with little to show for it. Exercise physiologists joined the search for the perfect form in the mid-1980s, hoping to scientifically extrapolate the ideal from the cloud of data in biomechanics. Their efforts have overwhelmingly failed. Runners with high bounce in their steps, shorter than average stride, or a meager toe launch often win gold medals over runners with more efficient running forms. It drives academics crazy.

This is because there's more to efficiency than meets the eye, and your body has a peculiar genius for finding it, regardless of the exotic dance it presents to the world. Crucial to efficient running, for example, is how much oxygen your heart can pump to muscles. Training improves this, but your unique heart faces unique limitations. The best trained athletes will eventually have to find speed and endurance from other body parts. Graciously, your body works out the details.

This doesn't mean that you should ignore your running form. Quite the opposite: watch the videos; stare at yourself. These images pour light into the changes training brings to your body. Injury, for example, often forces supporting muscles to compensate. Even as your injury heals, these muscles have overdeveloped, which may bring new inefficiencies to the way you run. Also, your form changes—not only over the years, but over the course of a workout or a race. Learning to keep your head up when fatigue sets in straightens your posture and ensures your lungs are getting adequate air, which forestalls collapse. Moving your arms forward and back at 90-degree angles (rather than cutting across your chest) conserves energy. When you hear your feet slapping on the pavement, muscle fatigue is making itself at home. It's time to knock off for the day.

The best way to maintain flawless form, however, is to mix up your workouts. Hill charges, sprints, high-stepping intervals, bounding (as if you were leaping from rock to rock), stadium stairs, skipping—yes, skipping—and trail running all put demands on muscles that tend to do subsidiary work in your normal workouts. Your body will wrench speed and strength from the crazy commotion. Over time, it will adapt your form to make the most of the challenge at hand. Training is ultimately about willful change to our bodies (and to who we are). It only makes sense that we should let our bodies have a say in these things. ∎

Distance carried forward: _____

5 Monday   278

_____

Where & When: _____ **Distance:** _____
Comments: _____
_____

6 Tuesday   279

_____

Where & When: _____ **Distance:** _____
Comments: _____
_____

7 Wednesday   280

_____

Where & When: _____ **Distance:** _____
Comments: _____
_____

8 Thursday   281

_____

Where & When: _____ **Distance:** _____
Comments: _____
_____

9 Friday   282

_____

Where & When: _____ **Distance:** _____
Comments: _____
_____

October

Saturday 10

Where & When: Distance:

Comments:

Sunday 11

Where & When: Distance:

Comments:

© CORBIS

tip: The difference between soreness and injury can be subtle. Any sharp, localized pain that doesn't stop as your running progresses and anything that alters your running form suggest injury.

Distance this week: Weight:

Distance carried forward:

12 Monday 285

Where & When: **Distance:**

Comments:

13 Tuesday 286

Where & When: **Distance:**

Comments:

14 Wednesday 287

Where & When: **Distance:**

Comments:

15 Thursday 288

Where & When: **Distance:**

Comments:

16 Friday 289

Where & When: **Distance:**

Comments:

October

Saturday 17

Where & When: Distance:

Comments:

Sunday 18

Where & When: Distance:

Comments:

© Tim Tadder/CORBIS

tip: If fatigue persists for two days after a hard workout, chances are you're overtraining. Dial it back. Get some rest.

Distance this week: **Weight:**

Distance carried forward:

19 Monday   292

Where & When: Distance:

Comments:

20 Tuesday   293

Where & When: Distance:

Comments:

21 Wednesday   294

Where & When: Distance:

Comments:

22 Thursday   295

Where & When: Distance:

Comments:

23 Friday   296

Where & When: Distance:

Comments:

October

Saturday 24

Where & When: Distance:

Comments:

Sunday 25

Where & When: Distance:

Comments:

© Patrik Giardino/CORBIS

tip: Contrary to the computer display on your treadmill, there is no such thing as a "fat burning zone." High-intensity exercise burns fat calories as well as carbohydrate calories. Your body doesn't get to choose which.

Distance this week: Weight:

Distance carried forward: _____

26 Monday 299

Where & When: _____ **Distance:** _____
Comments: _____

27 Tuesday 300

Where & When: _____ **Distance:** _____
Comments: _____

28 Wednesday 301

Where & When: _____ **Distance:** _____
Comments: _____

29 Thursday 302

Where & When: _____ **Distance:** _____
Comments: _____

30 Friday 303

Where & When: _____ **Distance:** _____
Comments: _____

304   **Saturday 31**

Where & When: **Distance:**

Comments:

305   **Sunday 1**

Where & When: **Distance:**

Comments:

tip:
Relax and shorten your stride on downhill patches. You're less likely to spill or provoke injury.

tip: Are you burning too much energy on a hill? Monitor your effort, not your speed.

tip: Pain that persists in a 2- to 6-inch area around your lower shin—even after a workout—may indicate shin splints.

Notes:

Distance this week: **Weight:**

November

SUNDAY	MONDAY	TUESDAY	WEDNESDAY	THURSDAY	FRIDAY	SATURDAY
1	2	3 Election Day (USA)	4	5	6	7
8	9	10	11 Veterans' Day (USA) Remembrance Day (Canada, UK)	12	13	14
15	16	17	18	19	20	21
22	23	24	25	26 Thanksgiving (USA)	27	28
29	30 St. Andrew's Day (UK)					

"Training gives us an outle
for suppressed energies created b
stress and thus tones the spirit just a
exercise conditions the body.

—Arnold Schwarzenegge

HARMONY

In those weeks when your workouts are sweet, cross training is about as appealing as cold oatmeal. Weights and whatnot steal time from running. They diffuse focus. They reveal athletic weaknesses. They hurt. To be sure, training of any kind is obnoxiously specific. If you want to get better at running, you have to run. And the worst time to begin cross training is when you're within reach of a running goal. Trouble is, most of us never discover cross training until we're sidelined by injury.

Here's a better time: immediately after you've succeeded or failed at a goal, especially a distance race. The day after presents an abyss—sweet or bitter. Either way, it's a great time to reassess. Cross training casts light into your next goal with its diversion alone. It allows running muscles to heal. It keeps your cardiovascular fitness where it needs to be. It builds supporting muscles, which can prevent running injuries. And it has the odd ability, when other goals are set aside, to bring gratification, even pleasure.

Instinct and fun should lead you to the type of cross training you do, though runners benefit most from strength training combined with cardio exercises. You've heard it before, but go slow with weights and resistance machines. Gradually build toward more repetitions, and even more gradually toward higher loads. Incidentally, you can use strength training to ward off running injuries to your hips, knees, and ankles by doing repetitions of hand-held weights while standing on one foot, using a balance ball—

or anything else that forces your proprioceptors to maintain your balance.

Almost any form of cardio exercise will have a lower impact on your body than running, so elliptical trainers, cross-country ski machines, rowing ergometers, bicycles (stationary and otherwise), aerobics classes, swimming, and water running all make excellent forms of cross training. If you have a heart-rate monitor, aim to work at or above 70 percent of your maximum rate, which is 220 minus your age. Roughly speaking, one hour at this intensity equals a five-mile run. But remember that you're using different muscle groups. It will take several weeks for muscles to match your aerobic fitness. Push them too fast, and you can hurt yourself.

And as for running? If you stop entirely, plan to reintroduce it into your workouts within two weeks, but limit your weekly mileage to about one-third of your regular training routine. Eliminate intervals, hill charges, and any other speed drills. This will maintain your fitness at a level that you can scale up quickly when you're seized by a new running goal. It allows your body to mend. And it prevents the shocking disappointment that comes with starting anew.

Invariably, you'll want to begin raising your running mileage—a splendid idea. Even a month or two of cross training will make you a stronger runner, a more agile athlete. So let running begin to crowd out the cardio you're doing. As the term implies, cross training is ultimately about finding the maximum benefits from all your efforts. ■

Distance carried forward:

2 Monday   306

Where & When: **Distance:**

Comments:

3 Tuesday   307

Where & When: **Distance:**

Comments:

4 Wednesday   308

Where & When: **Distance:**

Comments:

5 Thursday   309

Where & When: **Distance:**

Comments:

6 Friday   310

Where & When: **Distance:**

Comments:

November

Saturday 7

Where & When: Distance:

Comments:

Sunday 8

Where & When: Distance:

Comments:

© Patrik Giardino/CORBIS

tip: You are most likely to get injured when you're new to running, when you're new to racing, when you increase your mileage, when you introduce speed work to your program, and when you're at the peak of your performance.

Distance this week: **Weight:**

Distance carried forward: _____

9 Monday   313

_____

_____

Where & When: _____ **Distance:** _____
Comments: _____

_____

10 Tuesday   314

_____

_____

Where & When: _____ **Distance:** _____
Comments: _____

_____

11 Wednesday   315

_____

_____

Where & When: _____ **Distance:** _____
Comments: _____

_____

12 Thursday   316

_____

_____

Where & When: _____ **Distance:** _____
Comments: _____

_____

13 Friday   317

_____

_____

Where & When: _____ **Distance:** _____
Comments: _____

_____

November

Saturday 14

Where & When: **Distance:**

Comments:

Sunday 15

Where & When: **Distance:**

Comments:

© Chase Jarvis/CORBIS

tip: On long inclines, work your arms harder; it helps.

Distance this week: **Weight:**

Distance carried forward:

16 Monday 320

Where & When: Distance:

Comments:

17 Tuesday 321

Where & When: Distance:

Comments:

18 Wednesday 322

Where & When: Distance:

Comments:

19 Thursday 323

Where & When: Distance:

Comments:

20 Friday 324

Where & When: Distance:

Comments:

325   Saturday **21**

Where & When: Distance:

Comments:

326   Sunday **22**

Where & When: Distance:

Comments:

© John Henley/CORBIS

tip: Even a half-hour run six days a week has proven as effective as drugs for fighting depression.

Distance this week: Weight:

Distance carried forward:

23 Monday 327

Where & When: Distance:
Comments:

24 Tuesday 328

Where & When: Distance:
Comments:

25 Wednesday 329

Where & When: Distance:
Comments:

26 Thursday 330

Where & When: Distance:
Comments:

27 Friday 331

Where & When: Distance:
Comments:

November

Saturday **28**

Where & When: **Distance:**

Comments:

Sunday **29**

Where & When: **Distance:**

Comments:

© Chase Jarvis/CORBIS

tip: Lose the ankle weights, which hinder form and often cause injury. Instead, do hill charges to strengthen your legs.

Distance this week: **Weight:**

Distance carried forward: _____

30 Monday 334

Where & When: _____ Distance: _____

Comments: _____

1 Tuesday 335

Where & When: _____ Distance: _____

Comments: _____

2 Wednesday 336

Where & When: _____ Distance: _____

Comments: _____

3 Thursday 337

Where & When: _____ Distance: _____

Comments: _____

4 Friday 338

Where & When: _____ Distance: _____

Comments: _____

339 _____ **Saturday 5**

_____

Where & When: _____ **Distance:** _____

Comments: _____

_____

340 _____ **Sunday 6**

_____

Where & When: _____ **Distance:** _____

Comments: _____

_____

tip:

Introduce no more than one new training element—hills, distance, speed—per week.

tip: Wind dehydrates—both in summer and in winter. Hydrate accordingly.

tip: Make time in your workouts for one slow run a week. It teaches pace and patience.

Notes: _____

_____

_____

Distance this week: _____ **Weight:** _____

December

SUNDAY	MONDAY	TUESDAY	WEDNESDAY	THURSDAY	FRIDAY	SATURDAY
		1	2	3	4	5
6	7	8	9	10 Human Rights Day	11	12 First day of Hanukkah
13	14	15	16	17	18	19 Last day of Hanukkah
20	21	22	23	24 Christmas Eve	25 Christmas Day	26 Kwanzaa begins (USA) Boxing Day (Canada, Australia—NSW, QLD, VIC) St. Stephen's Day (Eire)
27	28 Boxing Day (NZ, UK, Australia—ACT, NT, TAS, WA) Proclamation Day (Australia—SA)	29	30	31		

" Courage is not the absence of fear, but simply moving on with dignity despite fear."

—Pat Riley, Miami Heat coach

DETRAINING

Why fight the cheer of the holiday season? Deep winter makes a fitting time to stop your workouts, to let the body mend. Hole up with friends and family. Refocus your priorities. Throw another log on the fire; enjoy the playoffs.

And watch your body fall apart.

Detraining is a rude surprise, as anyone who has been sidelined by injury knows. Exercise physiologists have only recently turned their attention to the opposite end of training. Roughly speaking, three months of not running will give you the same cardiovascular fitness as someone who has lived off delivery pizza, TV remote in hand for the past 10 years, even without the weight gain. Are you depressed yet?

With training, your body produces greater volumes of blood plasma, which is mostly water, the better to carry oxygen to your hungry muscles. When you stop running, you lose that water (which greatly accounts for the weight you shed when you stop working out). Also, your heart pumps less blood to the nether regions of your body. In shocking short order, the running muscles you've spent months—even years—building work with much less efficiency. They fatigue more quickly. Within weeks, you lose your fitness.

Physiologists are puzzled by why this happens so quickly. Equally mysterious is why athletes regain lost ability so fast. And this is the silver lining of detraining. Runners can typically return to their peak performance in a fraction of the time it took them to attain it in the first place. It's almost as if your muscles had memory. More likely, training makes permanent changes to your body—in nerve-firing patterns, blood vessels, and even the number of mitochondria in your cells. These seem to go dormant when you do, then kick in when training resumes. It's also possible that after years of running, you train smarter. You know how to get the most from each workout.

Whatever the explanation, you don't have to start from scratch when you return from the holidays, even if the first several workouts will certainly feel like it. Of course, the longer you languish on the sofa, the longer it will take you to return to your old performance. Also, you lose resiliency with age. It may take 10 days to get back to 25 miles a week when you're 25. It'll take longer when you're 55.

A better scheme is to avoid detraining altogether. Instead, reduce the number and length of your workouts during the holiday season. Focus on intensity. The best research shows that you can retain most of your speed and endurance with less than half the miles you typically run if you replace those miles with intervals, tempo runs, hill charges, and other types of speed work. You can't sustain these types of workouts forever (and you may injure yourself if you do). So don't be afraid to stop running entirely. Just remember that the longer the holiday party, the meaner the hangover that awaits you when you return. ∎

Distance carried forward:

7 Monday 341

Where & When: **Distance:**

Comments:

8 Tuesday 342

Where & When: **Distance:**

Comments:

9 Wednesday 343

Where & When: **Distance:**

Comments:

10 Thursday 344

Where & When: **Distance:**

Comments:

11 Friday 345

Where & When: **Distance:**

Comments:

December

Saturday 12

Where & When: Distance:

Comments:

Sunday 13

Where & When: Distance:

Comments:

© Uli Wiesmeier/zefa/CORBIS

tip: If you're planning to get in shape after the holidays, begin four weeks before. Even if you slack off when they arrive, you'll have a great aerobic base to begin doing real work when the new year begins.

Distance this week: **Weight:**

Distance carried forward: _____

14 Monday   348

Where & When: _____   Distance: _____
Comments: _____
_____

15 Tuesday   349

Where & When: _____   Distance: _____
Comments: _____
_____

16 Wednesday   350

Where & When: _____   Distance: _____
Comments: _____
_____

17 Thursday   351

Where & When: _____   Distance: _____
Comments: _____
_____

18 Friday   352

Where & When: _____   Distance: _____
Comments: _____
_____

December

Saturday **19**

Where & When: Distance:

Comments:

Sunday **20**

Where & When: Distance:

Comments:

© Jason Horowitz/zefa/CORBIS

tip: Pain and pleasure should guide stretching. Gently pull a muscle just until it tingles with pain, then stop. Also, no ballistic stretches (i.e. bouncing); these provoke injury.

Distance this week: **Weight:**

Distance carried forward:

21 Monday   355

Where & When: Distance:

Comments:

22 Tuesday   356

Where & When: Distance:

Comments:

23 Wednesday   357

Where & When: Distance:

Comments:

24 Thursday   358

Where & When: Distance:

Comments:

25 Friday   359

Where & When: Distance:

Comments:

December

Saturday **26**

Where & When: Distance:
Comments:

Sunday **27**

Where & When: Distance:
Comments:

© Anthony West/CORBIS

tip: Strength is developed not during the workout, but during the period your body rests. Take rest seriously, even extravagantly.

Distance this week: Weight:

Distance carried forward:

28 Monday 362

Where & When: **Distance:**

Comments:

29 Tuesday 363

Where & When: **Distance:**

Comments:

30 Wednesday 364

Where & When: **Distance:**

Comments:

31 Thursday 365

Where & When: **Distance:**

Comments:

1 Friday

Where & When: **Distance:**

Comments:

Dec/Jan 2010

Saturday 2

Where & When: _____ Distance: _____

Comments: _____

Sunday 3

Where & When: _____ Distance: _____

Comments: _____

tip:

Running with a cold? First do a neck check. If it's a head cold (above the neck), go ahead with your workout. If the virus has settled in your chest (below the neck), skip your run and rest.

tip: If you begin shivering 10 minutes into a run, seek shelter immediately. In all likelihood, you have a fever.

tip: On slippery terrain, shorten your stride.

Notes: _____

_____

_____

Distance this week: _____ Weight: _____

Twelve Months of Running

Jan. 5	Jan. 12	Jan. 19	Jan. 26	Feb. 2	Feb. 9	Feb. 16	Feb. 23	March 2	March 9	March 16	March 23	March 30

To create a cumulative bar graph of weekly mileage,
apply an appropriate scale at the left-hand margin.
Then fill in the bar for each week of running.

	Apr. 6	Apr. 13	Apr. 20	Apr. 27	May 4	May 11	May 18	May 25	June 1	June 8	June 15	June 22	June 29

To create a cumulative bar graph of weekly mileage,
apply an appropriate scale at the left-hand margin.
Then fill in the bar for each week of running.

July 6	July 13	July 20	July 27	Aug. 3	Aug. 10	Aug. 17	Aug. 24	Aug. 31	Sept. 7	Sept. 14	Sept. 21	Sept. 28

To create a cumulative bar graph of weekly mileage,
apply an appropriate scale at the left-hand margin.
Then fill in the bar for each week of running.

| Oct. 5 | Oct. 12 | Oct. 19 | Oct. 26 | Nov. 2 | Nov. 9 | Nov. 16 | Nov. 23 | Nov. 30 | Dec. 7 | Dec. 14 | Dec. 21 | Dec. 28 |

A Record of Races

Date	Place	Distance	Time	Pace	Comments & Excuses

A Record of Races

Date	Place	Distance	Time	Pace	Comments & Excuses

The 10K

Pace is crucial. And you won't magically find it on race day. If you've resisted using a stopwatch or a heart monitor in your workouts, training for a 10K race is the perfect opportunity to abandon those prejudices.

Divide the race into three equal segments and start slower than you want. Don't reach your race pace until the second segment. Push on the third. But your times between these three segments shouldn't vary by more than 10 percent.

Warm up? Yes, even a slow half-mile run before the race is likely to improve your performance, not fatigue you. Remember that a 10K event is too short to grant you a sufficient warm-up during the race.

The Half Marathon

If you're running a half-marathon as preparation for a marathon, cut your weekly long run to no more than 12 miles and raise the pace.

Don't be shaken by early mistakes. If you go out too fast, for example, simply dial back as soon as you recognize your error. It's a long race and there's plenty of time to recover from just about any kind of blunder.

Every week should include three types of workouts: speed drills, tempo runs, and your long run. Speed drills make you faster. Tempo runs raise your lactate threshold, which will help you maintain a racing pace in the second half of the event. And your weekly long run increases endurance. Toss in some cross training when time allows.

The Marathon

No one masters the marathon. Anything can happen on its long tortuous course, which is why it is such a seductive and exciting event. It's in your interest to arrive at the starting line with this humility.

> *Believe it or not, it's better to undertrain than to overtrain. What you haven't developed by race day can sometimes be overcome with adrenalin and desire. For an overtrained runner, the race is over before it starts.*

Seek support. Train with a partner or a running group. Get your loved ones to cheer you on at the race. Raise money for a cause. The road to the marathon can be long and lonely. Let others help you get there.

The Triathlon

Rehearse transitions. Without specific training, it takes bicycling legs longer to reach their running stride than many athletes realize. Pulling dry socks onto wet feet can be an ordeal. Fussing with uncooperative equipment squanders time.

> *Your weakest event deserves the greatest amount of training effort. Sorry, it's true. Most triathletes use their best event to make up time. The better strategy is not to lose time in your weak event.*

Get used to crowding. In open water where visibility is often poor, contact with other swimmers is inevitable. On bicycles it can be dangerous. Patience pays. Fighting through a pack of competitors wastes energy and can throw your race into jeopardy. Relax. Your opportunity to pass will come.

JANUARY 2010

_____
_____
_____
_____
_____

FEBRUARY 2010

_____
_____
_____
_____
_____

MARCH 2010

_____
_____
_____
_____
_____

APRIL 2010

_____
_____
_____
_____
_____

MAY 2010

_____
_____
_____
_____
_____

JUNE 2010

_____
_____
_____
_____
_____

JULY 2010

_____
_____
_____
_____
_____

AUGUST 2010

_____
_____
_____
_____
_____

SEPTEMBER 2010

_____
_____
_____
_____
_____

OCTOBER 2010

_____
_____
_____
_____
_____

NOVEMBER 2010

_____
_____
_____
_____
_____

DECEMBER 2010

_____
_____
_____
_____
_____